From

Ken

Christmas 2018

Route 66
and
Its Sorrows

Also by Carolyn Miller

Light, Moving
After Cocteau

Chapbooks
World Made of Desire
This Is Mine
Constant Lover
The Reluctant Dinner Guest

Route 66
and
Its Sorrows

Carolyn Miller

Terrapin Books

Terrapin Books
4 Midvale Avenue
West Caldwell, NJ 07006

www.terrapinbooks.com

ISBN: 978-0-9976666-5-6
LCCN: 2016958603

First Edition

Cover art: *Missouri Woods, Spring No. 1*, Carolyn Miller,
acrylic on paper

For Dave

Contents

Traveling Toward Avalon

Early Beauty

Route 66 and Its Sorrows

October already, the mornings dark and rain coming back
like the past, people and places I thought I had forgotten:

the unknown boy who flung himself across the room to kiss me,
the girls who ate sardines out of the can, the one who dove headfirst

through the open window of a car, the roller rink that played
"Your kisses take me to Shangri-La." *The past is never dead,*

someone in Faulkner said, *it isn't even past.* For here we are,
riding at night in an open convertible in the rain, laughing

as if we understood, while around us stretch the years to come,
unthinkable and undreamed.

Red-Winged Blackbirds

Cold water in the springhouse,
mint and watercress in the blue-black spring;
signs carved in the cave up in the bluff,
arrowheads in the new-plowed field.
Narrow beds in the sitting room,
dark velvet and glass cases in the parlor;
jars of jewel colors in the cellar,
tin ladle in a chipped tin bowl of water,
dinner bell on the porch. Small
angels of memory spread black wings
with blood-red shields,
leave the earth and rise as one,
flying over the corn.

Photograph, 1912

Three years before he went to harness the horse,
before the horse reared in the stall,
before the boy was shoved into the nail
protruding from the wall, before he lay
in the farmyard dirt, blood trickling
from his ears, the littlest boy, the Uncle John
I would never know, looked at the camera,
trying not to laugh.

Son of Big Piney

In the photo he is almost as thin as the fence posts
he stands in front of, his skin as dark as an Indian's, and
he wears a tight jacket buttoned up to the neck and a felt hat
with a big flat brim. He looks like a boy in a shtetl, but instead

he is on the old farm at Big Piney. Someone has taken his picture
by surprise, someone who has just bought or been given
the kind of camera that took small, narrow snapshots
like this one, with a white scalloped border. His eyes

stare out at the camera, alarmed, with so much white showing
they look like the eyes of a frightened horse. *Isn't that
a terrible picture?* one of the aunts would whisper, many
years later. And I wondered why this man who became my father,

a man who grew round and fleshy and red in the face, why he kept
this creased photo of himself as a shockingly thin, dark, feral boy,
working the fence line, surrounded by horses and Holsteins, silage
and chickens and deer and cornfields, manure and catfish

and bullfrogs and crickets, lightning bugs and snakes and the barn
and the springhouse and the ice-cold spring, and the Big Piney River,
flowing in its summer beauty toward the Gasconade.

1935

Morning in Bloodland, the McCourtneys' cabin.
My mother pulls her cloche hat down
over her bobbed black hair. She is wearing
her long skirt and middy blouse and thick
flesh-colored cotton stockings, held up with
elastic garters. My brother sits on his cot
and looks out on the fields of his life to come.
He is still too young to pray for happiness.

Dundas School

In the one-room schoolhouse: lice,
stink of wool, stink of bodies,
wood smoke from the iron stove.
My mother, her coarse black hair in a bob,
fixes the children with her amber-
colored eyes. A wooden cabin
by the river, the Roubidoux singing
its constant inconstant song:
All this will be swept away
and nothing will remain, except
some yellowed papers and the word
Dundas on a map, not even
a photograph of the children,
peering into the future in surprise.

Early Beauty

My mother has given me her linen dresses.
Years now they have hung empty-breasted
in the upstairs closet,
beside my dirty Easter bunnies
and the vanishing mothballs,
soft, thin linen, the colors of dyed eggs
and seashells—pale cream,
clear pink, the lightest
lavender—their texture almost like skin,
becoming more and more refined
as the world outside them grew coarser.
    Short-sleeved, fitted dresses with bust darts,
they are carefully made, with hidden snaps
and hooks and eyes, with shoulder pads
and hand-stitched pocket trim. All of them
emphasize the hips and the curve
of the lower back, and now they fit me.
I never could have imagined it—I
who once waited on Sunday morning, overwhelmed
by my lack of understanding,
in my blue-gray princess-line coat
and my straw hat with the cherries,
my mother the same age as I am now.
    I remember her then: broad-backed, her thick
coal-black hair chopped off at the nape,
her eyebrows dark and fierce
as those of any goddess. She is wearing linen,
seamed stockings, white summer heels
with a design of small holes;

she walks toward the old green car,
carrying hyacinths, tulips, daffodils
coaxed from the earth and gathered
to place before the altar,
flowers brilliant as a victory torch.

Summer Rain

All of a sudden: gold to green,
warm to cool—it's raining, and my mother runs
awkwardly, in housedress and apron,
to the clothesline, unpins the sheets and towels,
piles them in the basket, hurries them through
the screen door, perfumed with rain.
Spotted dog curled in his small house,
the birds gone silent. Rain in waves
across the hills and on the roof.
Outside my room up in the trees,
water music, dance of leaves.

Oh years, faces, strawberry patch, lilac
bush, summer rain.

Early June, the Ozarks

The day closes down; blue haze rises from the hills
across the valley. The airport signal light

comes on. Down on the river, mist rises from the water.
The cows begin their slow way across the fields

toward home. Now a deep wave of fragrance
starts welling up from the leaves and flowers.

Someone is calling hogs far-off, high and sweet,
and the birds gather in the trees, ecstatic.

The Journey of the Artist

Granddad Miller died in his house downtown, the dark
house with the player piano and the velvet piano scarf
and the cut-velvet pillows that said Mother, with a hedge apple tree

in front and a garden in back where I once found hundreds
of lettuce seedlings growing from a spilled package of seed,
and the well beside the house, and the big front porch

where Grandma Miller lay on a bed the summer before she died,
and Granddad's funeral was held in the Big Piney Baptist
     Church, one room
all made of wood, the chairs filled with people, and more
     standing in the back,

and more flowers than I'd ever seen, sprays of gladiolus and wreaths
of carnations supported on stands, and all the fat people sweating
and fanning themselves and the windows open, and my grandfather

lying in his wooden casket, small and trim and straight
as ever, wearing his thick white mustache and a black wool suit,
and we sang "The Old Rugged Cross" and "I Won't Have to Cross

Jordan Alone," and I saw my father's face collapse for the first
and last time in my life, and I sat, amazed, to know that he could weep,
and I understood then, as the flowers opened wider in the heat and kept

pouring out their death smell, that all of us in that room, my father
and mother and brother, and my aunts and my uncles, and even me,
were going to die.

Rapture

When they said the world was coming to an end,
I thought about my brother, his long limbs,
his good shoulders and thick hair, his small
white teeth, his beautiful feet at the end
of the hospital bed. How he lies now,
hazel eyes closed, in a metal coffin
embossed with dogwood blossoms. They said
the true believers would be taken up;
first my brother in his dark blue suit and all
the other dead in Christ, then the living,
would ascend to meet Jesus in the air.
But I remembered how my brother and I
already had been raptured,
how each year we were caught up
in spring, reborn again as the flowers
were reborn: first the hawthorn and wild plum,
pale glimmerings among the leafless trees,
then the violets and honeysuckle,
the redbud and the dogwood, those thick,
creamy cross-shaped flowers pierced
and rusted on the edges, held in rafts of bloom
all through the woods, until we were transformed,
taken up into the bodies of the flowers,
even as we stood, unmoving,
on a rocky hill.

The Door

A door opened: my brother walked through. He left
everything behind: his record collection, his road maps
to heaven, his coffee beans, the old books and dishes,
the walnut trees. He has gone off
without a bell or a lantern, in his best suit, into darkness.
Until the angry father calls him home,
welcoming him at last.

One Thousand, Two Thousand

When a storm swept over the far side
of the valley, above the airport signal tower,
I would run into the yard to dance as the light went green
and the clouds swelled and grew darker, filling the sky
with their roiling masses, and I whirled on the grass
beneath the walnut trees and their flying leaves.
And when the black sky was split by lightning
above the river valley and the Roubidoux and the cows
heading home, I stopped and counted—*one thousand, two thousand*—
before the thunder sounded, to see how far away the lightning was,
and when the first drops of rain splattered on the grass I ran
through it, leaping, while Sparky hid in the garage,
for I knew nothing about danger, about balls of fire that could enter
a house or a body, or how the world could suddenly
go wrong, or death race over the landscape,
riding the ridges and jumping the hollers, and I ran
in circles in the downpour until the storm passed off
to the east, over the drenched and steaming hills.

Dark, Starry, Sticky Night: Missouri

It's like falling into warm molasses, a dark
sweetness in which you can barely breathe; it's like
being drowned in blackness, thick and moving
in slow waves around you, while above you shine the steady
lights of stars, and around you flicker the floating,
intermittent lights of lightning bugs; the smell of flowers
grows even stronger on the warm tide of the night,
all of summer welling into a flood of fragrance and
a heavy mixture of sex and sorrow, and everywhere
cicadas and crickets are rasping out their brief sentient lives,
and off in the woods a whippoorwill keeps calling
that each moment is sweeter and more precious
than any you will ever taste again.

Dog Days

Late August, and the webworms build their gray clouds
in the trees. The dirt daubers' nests grow beneath the eaves.
Some wasps are trapped in the upstairs bedrooms,
angry in the ceiling fixtures; waves of heat radiate
from the wood and plaster. Fans are whirring in each room,
and moisture beads the ice tea pitcher. These are the dog days, when
some dogs go crazy, staggering down the bubbled blacktop roads,
foam dripping from their mouths. This is the death of summer, with
its shriveled leaves and smell of grass scorching in the sun.
We sleep in the basement with the mold and scorpions. The rivers shrink.
A pale green scum films the surface of the ponds, and brushfires break out
on the hills. At night, they glow as if the hills had cracked open to reveal
their burning hearts, as if this is how the world will end, first
the smell of far-off smoke, then the high wild flames.

Lost

Whatever happened to my Eisenhower jacket,
sized for a five-year-old, folded
in the mahogany dresser in the cold upstairs room?
And where is the white rabbit-fur muff
with a red moiré taffeta lining
my mother kept in one of her dresser drawers?
I want them back, along with my mother's
forties hats and sunglasses and her linen dresses.
I want the lamb's wool sweater I wore in high school,
trimmed with pearls around the collar and the placket,
and I want that fur collar with velvet ties and pompoms
Beverly and Patsy gave me for my sixteenth birthday.
And still I am mourning my formal for the junior prom,
dance length and strapless, white with a red cummerbund,
but most of all I want the French heels that went with it—
white Springolators, backless and toeless, with a red bow—
that sprang me out of the place I hated,
the place I took with me when I left, the place
that stays with me everywhere I go.

Cigarettes

My best friend taught me to inhale
as we sat at my open bedroom window
trying to blow the smoke outside
to the walnut trees and the Ozark night.
My father sat downstairs in his brown
vinyl chair, reading the Bible, enclosed
in a red cloud of rage. Upstairs,
I drew the burning smoke into my lungs,
coughing and taking in the poison
that would fill me again and again
in the years to come.

Three Weeks After

the funeral in the funeral home
my mother thought was so nice, with its
gold shag carpet and low swirled-plastic ceiling,
the metal folding chairs, the plastic sculptures
on the walls, the lights that looked like fake
Egyptian funerary urns on either side of my father's
metallic vaultlike coffin,
I dreamed that I was running away from people
who wanted to stab me with long needles,
and I ran on all fours like an animal
so I could go faster, first extending my arms
straight, well in front of me, then propelling
my body forward and swinging my bent legs up
under me and pushing hard with them until I came
to the frozen-over San Francisco Bay,
even the waves frozen in place, and gray
sheets of ice stretching to the horizon, the beach
covered with snow, and I ran along it until I came
to a highway, like the highway
I had walked along in Missouri
to see my father's grave. In my dream,
snow covered the highway and formed
a long tunnel filled with snow stalactites;
in reality, the road was clear, though snow was heavy
on the shoulders, where it had hardened to a crust,
and on the ground in the cemetery,
where it was smooth and deep, and where,
under a mound of dirt and frozen flower sprays, lay
my old enemy.

December in Missouri

Sound carries over the snow, down to the river
gone low in the cold. The valley covered

with a white veil; the cows, dark smudges,
move across it, going home. Brilliant birds

cluster in the trees, bittersweet burns
among bare gray branches. The frozen grass

creaks beneath my feet. Sound of my breath
entering and exiting my lungs.

Oh my dead father, my mother, my brother
under a new white blanket. And the earth spinning
under the winter stars.

Back Home

I was alone in the old house, emptying out
the drawers. There in the buffet, in the dining room,
where he used to keep his Sen-Sen and
his wide collection of working and nonworking flashlights,
was my father's gun. Not his gun, but my grandfather's
or great-grandfather's gun, the one I'd heard about
for years, the one my father used to take out in the car
with him when he made house calls, then hid somewhere
in the garage. Not a Luger, after all, but a Mauser,
wooden handled and antique. So I aimed it at the floor
and pulled the trigger, and was stunned to hear
the hard, flat sound of an explosion in my ears, to smell
the peppery gunpowder smell, to see the long brown scar
the bullet dug in my mother's carpet. Yes,
it's me again, still here, still doing something wrong.

Lesson

I took what I was given, first without question,
later with surprise: the strange family, the hills,
the old desert religion and its blood sacrifice.

Next came books and wanderings
among the trees; snow and flowers and moons were given
and then taken, but they promised to return, and did.

Yet some things were taken back for good: the yellow cats,
a spotted dog, the old road through the woods.
And then the roll call of the taken grew: awkward aunts

and silent uncles, the tall brother, the diminished parents—
the taking back of each universe I thought

would last forever. Faces and rooms, my teachers, friends—
gifts that won't return, unlike the snow and moons
and flowers, not even when those too have passed away.

Things I Left Behind

I thought I'd left them there,
the empty Mason jars, the cast-iron pans,
the old suitcases, but they're with me still,
the big green chair that disappeared, the one
I used to sit behind on the floor, reading
the Bobbsey Twins, the old player piano
with its alligatored skin that the new piano teacher
looked inside to find a rat's nest of torn paper
that must have dated back fifty years, the turtles
courting death to cross the blacktop road,
the leeches my brother picked from my legs
at the swimming hole, the copperhead
I stepped on up on the river, the applesauce cakes
and gooseberry pies, the boiled beef tongue
still with its nubbly skin and severed veins,
the dirt daubers and the webworms,
chipmunks and chickadees, the preachers
telling us that everything was sinful, especially us,
born stained with sin upon the earth, and how
we had to be redeemed, the sink pumps and
the baby chicks, the bantam hens, the poorhouse
on the spring road and the coonhounds baying
in the valley, the cows walking slowly home across
the pasture, and the man calling hogs at the end of day,
calling them so sweetly, as if calling down
the sun, as if calling up the katydids and bullfrogs
and the whippoorwills.

Street Trees of San Francisco

Third Day of the Year

The new year starts off bravely, light
around its edges: Persimmons grow translucent

in a bowl. The hills are green; gray whales—
pregnant females first—leap and plunge their way

to Mexico. Juncos, down from Oregon, fatten
in backyards, while ginkgo trees release their hoard of gold.

This early, we are hopeful—even the orange-bellied newts
crossing busy roads, sure they will find love.

January

I wasn't with my mother when she died.
Now I wonder: Do her flower bulbs still bloom each spring?

Toward the end, her voice on the phone so breathy
I could barely understand her words.

All our sorrows fade in unexpected winter sun;
even the hills curve up to meet its warmth.

See the startling colors of the moment,
how they accept everything that is.

Long before we were born it was the same:
the burning and the fading and the light's return.

Wild Poppies

California poppies everywhere in the community garden, especially on the hill just for native plants, as if drawn there by cream cups and lupine, wild irises and one lone mariposa lily. All nurtured by us, the garden volunteers—and the poppies are volunteers as well, as are the tiny bumblebees wallowing in pollen. When I wondered how the poppies knew to flock here, Vicki said she believed that flowers could talk. And I thought: Or they might murmur, or they might sing, like whales: *We want to live! We want to live!* Like Marilyn, who told me, toward the end, about the rush of gratitude she felt each morning when she woke to see the light coming through her curtains. Until the morning when she didn't wake, when she died without ever seeing Italy. Not Rome in summer, people sitting with their feet in the Fountain of the Sinking Boat, alongside the flower seller's roses. Or Venice in the spring, wisteria everywhere, its death-in-life, life-in-death flower falls, its baroque *escaliers*, its aria: *You are here, alive with us; drink deep of this perfume.*

Mount Oread

for Marilyn

Didn't we meet on the only hill in Kansas,
you of the long hair and the beautiful shoes,
me of the matching name and half-formed hopes?
And weren't we oreads, mountain nymphs,
living in the freshman dorm,
putting on lipstick in front of the built-in mirror,
walking the campus in a dream of youth,
and didn't the fields of Kansas stretch out around us
on all sides, flat and treeless in the Midwest summer,
sun-struck plains that reached into a future
we would never understand.

In the Headlands

Deep in the hollows of the hills covered with low-growing
thickets of chaparral spring freshets are sluicing down creases
and filling the cracks and the crevices matted with
dove-colored grass where dried corms and seeds collected in layers
all through the summer and insects leapt and the deer flattened
their beds in the tall yellow grass and the rains beat down storm
after storm all winter and winter stars moved in glittering file
overhead and the fog crept up from the ocean and wind tore
at the rough furze and even the mountain lions and the coyotes
slept in their dens yet now the green grass is springing up out of the old
in a sticky brilliance and harsh yellow trumpets of sorrel
are sounding and the whips of the willows have reddened and
wild irises blue the flanks of the hills and down
in the deepest folds and the dank marshes of bottomland
stands of calla lilies have slowly unfolded their heavy white spathes
to reveal their tall golden spadices stiff with blossom and thick
with pollen

Sunny Morning, February

And then I realized that spring was here, that the plum
trees and tulip trees and acacias had been blooming for weeks
in the cold and the fog,

and though it was late, Chinese New Year
was almost here, and for a while, maybe no one else I loved
would die, so I should go out

and make my way among the people
buying pomelos and quince blossoms, feeling the sun on my face
both for myself and for those who no longer could,

and I walked out into my ghost-filled city,
and it shone.

A Walk to the Bay

Blue mist rises from the water
like the blue haze over Ozark hills
at the end of a summer day.
No wild sweet peas yet. Remember
how women grew sweet peas to climb up strings
on the sides of porches, not far
from the four-o'clocks? And how
people used to sit out in what they called
the cool of the evening until night fell,
and the birds finally quieted down? And as if
at a signal, fragrance began to pour out
of the throats of countless flowers and the pores
of the leaves, and sweetness rose from the earth
and filled the darkness. And slowly the random
floating lights of lightning bugs began to appear,
and the knowledge of beauty and its claim on you
began to beat in your chest, as if tears
were filling a cup until the weight of them
overflowed, because you knew even then
you would leave that place.

To Dave

The last time I saw you, you were still a boy.
Your hair was short; light fell on your face and on
the beautiful musculature of your arms.
Your green eyes were the large eyes
of a boy, and your skin was the golden color
it turned in the sun. My suitcases
were already packed for the rest of my life,
but it never occurred to me that I would lose you utterly;
that I would never run into you on the street again
under the first, still-shiny leaves of summer.

End of May

There was my heart, which closed and hardened
like a black walnut when the green hull
darkens. There was the fire-in-the-bush,
blooming because it was spring. Later came
the wave of sorrow, a desperate kind of blue,
when I understood what I had done.

RSVP

Did you receive my invitation?
I sent it by starlight and by leaves.
I sent it on the autumn air a day ago.
I asked you to come back, just as you were,
golden, with green eyes. I have sent
this invitation more than once,
by the sound of foghorns, in a stratus cloud.
You may not have received it
where you are, in another world.
But if you are looking out your window
at the past, if you remember the arrogant girl
who let you go, look for my invitation.
I sent it by red-winged blackbird, then
by redbird, then by whippoorwill.
I sent it by honeysuckle, dogwood,
redbud. I sent it to you disguised as a dream.
Then I sat and waited for you by the door,
watching through the window just
to see you walking toward me
one more time.

Spring, San Francisco

and the old cat sleeps
curled into himself,
fur the color of fog.
Firecrackers explode
in the dark of the moon,
someone sweeping up
plum blossoms,
small birds clustered
in the trees.
Walking through North Beach,
sidewalks wet, I remember
different storefronts,
different days.
We ate and drank,
laughed and danced,
walked home down Grant,
morning leaking from the bay.
Bottles in the streets,
salt in the air,
and coffee roasting;
cigarettes and Lysol,
wine and garlic,
another strange
bed left behind
and years ahead,
for we had nothing then
but time.

Walking Song

Everything flaming everything flowering
everything dying inch by inch
mourning doves back for the season and calling
the new year gone older and moon growing thinner
quince blossoms open and plum petals falling
streets filled with red shreds of firecracker paper
the intricate city of getting and wanting
everything sinking everything floating
the earth underneath us trembling and shifting
spring racing past leaving us blinking
ablaze in the glittering light

Street Trees of San Francisco

Crab apple trees blooming all over town!
Some brave, hopeful soul in the street-tree
department has ordered them planted
on tired boulevards and wind-blasted avenues,
in the sad alleys and on dusty side streets:
little staked stick trees lined up and blossoming,
red mallow/rose madder/magenta to
candy pink, flamboyant pompoms dancing
alongside old ficuses—elephant-skinned
and struggling for balance—proud magnolias
and harum-scarum gum trees, gnarled pittosporums
smelling of jasmine, and—just in time
for the warm days of spring, and despite everything
that keeps going wrong—the ginkgos,
opening tiny green fans.

Time

for Susan

Could time end? scientists ask. The answer: Yes, and no.
Time's death might be abrupt or gradual, or time could be infinite,

they say, speaking cosmologically, not thinking of the small,
sure death of time that waits for each of us. Because of this

we cling to what we have, and are filled with appetite;
because of this, desire and longing drive us. Because of this,

my friend and I walk down by the bay, for the light that breaks
east of San Francisco, sedge and hemlock in the ditch

along the road, green rocks fallen from the cliff,
dolphins in the radiant water, the orange bridge aglow

in morning air, night herons in their hoods
up the pines, calla lilies sleeping on the hills.

You

The flowering crab trees and the wisteria almost
bloomed out, the rhododendrons in their giddy glory,
and us, carrying the dead. You who have vanished
into the air, whose spirit left your body in a fireball
or spiraled up like candle smoke, whose bones
lie under the ground or are burned
to fragments, we are carrying all that is left of you
whom we loved or didn't love, you
who walked with us, laughed with us, ate with us
in restaurants with straw-wrapped Chianti bottles,
drank cocktails in bars, danced drunkenly
to rock and roll. Memory flares at the edges—
how you looked that day, what you said or
didn't say—and you come back to us in dreams, confident,
animate with desire, as puzzling as you were in life.
You left us, slowly or in a hurry, taking so much with you:
whole chunks of our life that we don't remember, almost all
of yours that we never knew. Everything changes,
everything dies, everything's born again
in the Heraclitean fire. We who remain
hold out our arms. O you, who like our God,
are not there, we are here, we are carrying you.

Green and Hyde

Looking down on the building where I used to live, I saw the graveled roof where I had never been, afraid to climb the steep white ladder nailed against the wall. Inside my old flat, someone else was living in the space I had lived in for so long, and everything of mine was gone: the piano I couldn't play, the books I had and hadn't read. The narrow living room with the gas fireplace insert that didn't work was still there, the room where I had sat so many nights, first with my black cat, then my gray one. There was the bedroom, with its angled window, where I lay in bed to watch the sky and the redwood and the bamboo trees. And I saw how protected our lives had been, how we had lived like bees in our small compartments, how the honey of our days had been stored up amid the bitter smell of pollen, so that even the salt of our tears could not dissolve it; how our dreams and hopes had permeated plaster and lath and wood; and how even though my home had been repainted and reinhabited, it was all still there: what I had said and thought, what I had wanted and feared—it was there in the separate rooms, part of them now, and I was glad to know that from the back stairs you could still see the moon and the stars, and the transient planets moving among them, slow-dancing in the sky.

Why We Sleep

Vacation rental, Inverness, California

Because almost all the stew of spring
vegetables is gone; because only a spoonful of the homemade yogurt
brought from home remains; because
the fire is burning down, and the visitors have left on their long
drive back to the city; because
we have looked through every one of the pile of new books
on the table, and the words
in the ones we are reading are running together; because the lights
are going off across Tomales Bay,
and the land beneath us is floating quietly, and the coals fall
in the grate and the house
grows still, waiting for us to lie down in our unfamiliar beds;
because no cats come to us
with questions and demands; because even some flowers have closed
their eyes, and the apple blossoms
are resting; because the bakers are already sleeping so they can rise
at four to make our morning pastries;
because the fish are dreaming under the water, eyes open, rocking
in the incoming tide; because
our days ebb and flow like the tides outside these windows; because
we are practicing for death
in the midst of life; because the earth is carrying us, like a great boat,
toward the sun;
because the sun waits for us on morning's shore.

Traveling Toward Avalon

The Market in Limogne

I went back to the market but it was not the same,
because my friend was dead and I was looking at
all the beautiful things she could not see.
I knew she would have loved the bundled radishes,

the tutus and flamenco skirts of lettuces, the delicate
green beans and the women scooping up great handfuls
of them into their plastic bags. And the bottles of rosé,
blushing in the light, and the street that winds down

from the church where Mass was being held,
while outside we celebrated the Mass of artichokes
and cauliflowers, roasted pigs and curled dead quail
and newly dug potatoes, fragrant round cheeses

of Rocamadour and strange flattened peaches, dense
local cakes, jar after jar of pale foie gras, the rows
of bluely glistening mackerel, the giant tuna
with its black and ruby flesh, stolen from the sea.

For Nancy

I went to my garden today to dig up the crabgrass;
it's choking the roses and invading the nearby
community plots. I got a shovel out of the toolshed
and cleaned up most of one path and started around the roses,
but the soil is like rock there, thick with sideways crabgrass stems
and the roots they put down from their nodes. Soon I was pouring
with sweat, but I kept on digging, thinking of you and all the things
you loved: linen, beauty, French shoes, silly poems,
terrible puns, orchids, and always, roses. I remembered the deep well
of sorrow inside you for the bitterness of the world, along with your
fine understanding of how so much of life is folly.

I'll never get rid of this crabgrass; it keeps growing under the ground
where you can't see it except when it slants up out of the dirt, green
and jagged. Still, my roses are thriving: Cécile Brünner,
Blanc Double de Coubert, the fragile Heritage you gave me. I thought
    about how,
of all the months, you died in May, when roses were blooming everywhere:
Abraham Darby, flushed with pink and peach and coral; Fair Bianca,
with her scent of musk; Fragrant Cloud, to carry you on your way.

Ripeness

Thom and Julia's, Lucas Valley

Each year, in the fullness of summer, the stag
comes down through the golden grass
to eat our peaches at their moment of perfect ripeness.
How does he know before us, in our house
on the edge of open land, that the peaches are ripe?
It must be their fragrance on the wind, the aroma
of peach juice, that distillation of blossoms and sun,
swelling the dense, heavy flesh, straining
the sunset-mottled skin. So the stag
walks down the mountain through the dry canyons,
his hooves crushing wild oats and Indian paintbrush,
past the toyon and coyote bush and the buckeyes
casting their spiky fruit, to the edge of our yard,
where he thrusts his head with its wild candelabrum
over the fence and takes the peaches, one by one, into
his maw and crushes them with his ivory teeth
and swallows them, pulp and juice and pit. Then he turns
and steps his way slowly back up the mountain, leaving us a few
high-up peaches, and our yearly humbling.
For here is what we know: time and death, chagrin,
the limitations of knowledge. And here
is what he knows: the scent of humans, the silence
of mountain lions, the ache of hunger,
ripeness.

Late

Lord: it is time. The huge summer has gone by.
      —Rilke

Suddenly, it's late. Only yesterday: July, plums,
the first ripe blackberries. Then, one morning
the light changed, suddenly, it seemed, and for a moment
the scent of winter was in the air. Suddenly, though everything
has been changing infinitesimally every day: cells and stars
and molecules, the intricate system of our being.
Summer ending, the community garden slumbers under fog;
even the crows are away or asleep. The roses fulfill
their radiant destiny; the dahlias celebrate
in riotous color. Now the surprise lilies wither and twist
into black flames; the apples weigh down their branches.

This is my garden, fenced and wind-struck: fragile greenhouse,
hidden skunk den, raised beds. This is my city,
my winter house: uneven sidewalks, street trees,
smell of burning reefer drifting from the bus stop;
empty lot where Queen Anne's lace blooms in every phase
of its existence: green unfolding cages,
flushed pink spiky umbrels, starred canopies,
clutches of bouquets, feathery masses of miniature
white blossoms, some with the single
tiny purple flower in the center whose purpose
no one understands, the closed brown cages
rimmed with seeds just before they are released
into the end-of-summer air.

Autumnal Equinox

The elephant heart plums swing out on invisible orbits:
cold to hot, darkness to light. They disappear
like the moon; at the end of the summer,
they come back. Each one a universe, swollen on top,
tapered on end, a ghostly gray-green on the outside;
inside, a purple-red wound. They come here to tell us
to ripen, to abandon all caution, to give ourselves completely,
to rock with our heartbeats, to awaken like Buddha,
September vanishing in the fire.

Wait

Winter pansies in the market—soon, persimmons,
pomegranates. And I want to say, *No, wait.*

Stop taking us with you, you who have already
taken much. Let us stay just as we are

for a while. Let us have what we have.
Let the autumn roses bloom. Let the sun

keep burning off the fog each morning.
Let the grapes hang on the vines.
Let us stay a little longer in the slanting light.

What to Remember

How the blue arcs over us
by day; how night reveals
the long, looping spiral dance
of the universe.
How October brings
not just the slanting sun,
but the rare low blue fog,
drawn like tissue across the islands
in the bay.
How at night
light and the sounds of people
laughing, talking,
spill out of restaurants
onto the streets. How
the city hums and moans
around us,
the cared for
and the lost, the boy
prostitutes on Polk Street,
the men pushing everything they own
in shopping carts, the dead
gray surfaces of houses in
the Mission. How clouds
move through the bending blue:
stratus, cirrus, cumulus, nimbus,
buttermilk, clabber—and the low
rushing night clouds,
broken particles of fog,

race along with us,
part of our yearning and
our moments of
sudden joy. How meanwhile the trees
everywhere transpire,
connecting earth and sky;
and birds rise up into
rivers and whorls
of air, as below them
in the soil the bright sexual
bodies of flowers
are opening.
How, though nothing ever is
quite what we imagined,
how much we are given,
how the earth both clings to us
and holds us up.

The Barn House, Late October

Salmon Creek flowed past us, past the dune grass,
past the egrets and the reeds, but slowly,
it flowed deeply and slowly, like a meditation,
like a secret longing, it flowed so darkly
toward the ocean, which heaved its great blue body
at the shore. Wild ducks flew over the cottage,
calling to one another and to us, urgent cries
to follow them over the dunes and the water,
beyond the crests of lion-colored hills.
Over our heads in the dark, in the night,
the unseen Orionids flung themselves
through the atmosphere; a hail of stars
fell over the ocean as we lay sleeping
in our borrowed beds.

Environmental Poetry Festival

Rain outside the atrium, second of the season.
The veil thin today between the worlds, this one
with children clutching poems, and
the other one our friends have gone to because
we could not stop them. Dirty boots, wet feet, small smell
of coffee, groups of people trying to save the world,
Aiden cutting turtles from bright paper, gray light falling
from the skylight, light and shadow, rain
on the first day of November, falling as we are toward darkness,
taking the children and Halloween's leftover candy
with us. All Souls' Day tomorrow and the dead
already gathered, longing, in the shadows. Outside,
cars clog the Berkeley streets, poisoning the sky,
but the yards are full of flowers—bougainvillea
and belladonna, camellias browning at the edges—
and just today I read about the coho coming back
to California; a woman swimming in a remote creek up north
found schools of little fish among the rocks.

A long poem on blue paper on a long, gray afternoon,
haiku beating at the windows trying to get in. A man
with many missing teeth stops by my booth to tell me that
last year the waterfowl migration in the Central Valley was
unprecedented, something he thought all poets should be
aware of, and I agree; I want to go there to see them landing,
webbed feet thrust out to slap down on the water, then
the rocking resting, then the massive struggle of their outspread
beating wings and the sound they make
lifting their heavy bodies into sky.

Early November

The dead visited and fed again, sugar skulls
melting on the altars, marigolds wilting on the graves.
Not a cloud in the sky, smoke from the wildfires
vanished from the blackened hills, the year hanging on
to summer-autumn. How easily we could ascend
into that blue, its mix of threat and rapture—jack-o'-lanterns
rotting on the doorsteps, chrysanthemums sending out
their bitter scent, another year of our sweet life slipping from us,
moment by fiery moment.

Visitors

Everyone I've known is traveling toward me.
They crowd my dreams—the ones I didn't love

I love now in the night; the ones who didn't
love me seem benign, as if someday they might change.

The cold man who left me touches my bare foot secretly
with his bare foot beneath the table; the one

who drank himself to death comes back smiling,
with clear eyes. How could I know, when I was stumbling

through my life, that someday the other stumblers
would return for one more embrace, one more walk

along some lost street? The empty houses
of my dreams fill with visitors who vanished years ago,

and I am not surprised to see them now, our hair
still bright, our skin unlined, all our lives before us.

Now when I dream you,

you know me, not like those years
when you came to me in dreams
but didn't remember my face.
And I'm amazed to see you radiant with health,
not drinking yourself sick in some third-rate hotel;
your alcoholic-poet pallor is gone,
along with the bleached-blond hillbilly hooker
you took up with in some kind of revenge,
and so is your despair and your louche-life pals.
Best of all, none of that matters now;
you're with me in dreams, where we can't fail
each other the way we did in life, and your eyes are clear,
as if you've remembered what you taught me:
It's the poems that matter, however many we can make
and how we make them; what matters is
the songs we teach ourselves
to sing, however bitter, however ragged,
until there are no more songs, until
there are no more dreams and no more time.

Up on the River

for Dave

It's a picnic up on Granddad's farm.
Aunt Daisy's here, and Uncle Ches,
with his horses, Bill and Bob. My cat, Tangerine,
sleeps on the river rock that is the back-door step;
my dog, Sparky, chases chickens. It's hot;
the food is on a table underneath a tree,
covered with a cloth to keep the flies away.
Down by the spring my brother swings
on grapevines. My father sits in the shade,
his plate full of food; he's happy. My mother,
her hair black, brings a tall angel food cake
from the kitchen. And the spring is rising slowly,
icy water spilling out over the water moss
and watercress and mint, under the hickory trees,
the walnut trees, the sassafras. Even the first people
are here now, planting corn in the black dirt
of the river bottom, chipping out arrowheads,
drawing on the walls of the cave up in the bluff.
And you are here, in this place you never saw.
In the warm shade on the river bank
I touch your hard young arms, I look into your green
undisappointed eyes.

Late Turner

Doesn't it all fade,
aren't we all suffused with light
in this insubstantial pageant,
aren't we all in a painting by Turner,
burning and fading and rising up;
isn't it all a blur now: who we loved,
what we saw, where we walked
in the drama of light and air?
Even when we have fallen into the sea,
even after the ocean comes for us,
don't you know we stood and looked
in a shadowed room at blue spray,
and we were silent when we saw
that it was all rain and fire, ocean
and sky contesting and embracing,
that what were called studies
are emanations of the changing light
above tiny human figures lost
and wondering in the storm, and we saw
how, like him, we are caught in a tempest
pale and swirling and unfinished,
even though we tie ourselves to the mast
before it all dissolves, somehow
both sooner and later than
we were expecting.

Cosmology

*Time might lose its many attributes one by one. . .[It] may be
reduced to just another dimension of space, breaking the link between
cause and effect.*
    —from "Could Time End?" *Scientific American*, September 2010

Someday, time could be just a dimension of space, you read,
and suddenly you're back in the old kitchen,

and your father's making popcorn balls, or oyster stew
from oysters in a can. Your dog is still alive, and the Interstate

has not yet bypassed your town, or cut a huge gap in the hill
across the valley. Your mother still has her beautiful small teeth,

and day lilies are still blooming in her flower beds. What was it
you thought was happening then, the summer you made

your own stilts, the summer of the cowboy shirt
and the aqua jumper? Now time bends into space,

and you're sitting in a room in San Francisco, trying to peer
into a future when time will disappear and our earthly bodies

turn to suns, when our memories will become dark matter
and our dreams, dark energy.

Sunset on the 38 Geary

Each face staring straight ahead, no one speaking,
each rider holding the day carefully, like an egg,
past the piroshki bakeries, past the restaurants
selling *pho* and *bulgogi* and Shanghai dumplings
and *carnitas*, past the Church of the Star of the Sea
on the long blocks of the Outer Lands,
cement-covered sand dunes reaching out
to the Pacific and the blinding sunset light.
When the bus stops to let the people embark and
disembark, it makes a sound like baby wolves
howling at the moon. We drive on west, into
the sun. Each time the back door opens
it makes a sound like waterfowl
lifting from a lake. And we are hopeful,
even the old ones who struggle up the steps
to slowly ease into the seats reserved for them
and for the injured, and the young ones who think
they never will be old, for we believe that we will be delivered,
that we will be transported in our earthly bodies,
traveling as we are toward Avalon, the Island of the Blest,
with its golden apples and its lake of fire.

The Book of the Living

I looked out my window and saw
that the world was filled with light
in a city of wooden houses built
on hills. Around the edges, water
rocked and glinted, and a cloud of energy
expanded and condensed, changing shape.
I did not have the life I thought I wanted, but one
that surprised me every day, and it was
my life, crowded with words and sound, randomness
and emotion, everything a sign, a secret that
I could not understand, yet I knew
that beneath the blistered and peeling, shining
and faded surfaces, something I could not name
was binding us together despite our failures
and our imperfections; something to do with
longing, with desire, had set us spinning
and keeps us aloft, humming
in the darkness and the light.

Going Back to Big Spring

after Maurice Manning

When I go, I'll take the road down from the north,
over the creaky bridge—"where the prairie meets the hills"—
into Versailles, pronounced just the way it's spelled, wooden slats
rattling beneath the tires, river visible through the cracks
between the slats. Or I could take the highway that turns off
onto a narrow blacktop road, the one where on a summer evening,
a traveler is enveloped in the sudden sweet, heavy atmosphere
of another country: rivers, creeks, leaves, flowers, hills. Sooner or later
I might pass through Iberia, that wide place in the road
where someone lived though who it was I can't remember—
Aunt Ida? Uncle Levi?—past green glass insulators on the phone lines,
daisies and black-eyed Susans by the road. Or I could go by
Evening Shade, or Plato—even Palace, where Aunt Daisy ran
the P.O. in a little store built onto the house, a field in back
with Uncle Ches's horse named either Bill or Bob, not far
from the road to Granddad's farm. You can't go through Cookville
anymore; it's a ghost town now, and so is Bloodland, where my mother
rode her horse to school. I wouldn't use the Interstate, just
old Route 66, a lost road gleaming black in the folded green.
West through Buckhorn, east through Devil's Elbow,
where a witch lived in a cabin by the bridge, deeper
and deeper into the hills, crossing rivers threading through
the limestone, honeycombed—Big Piney, Little Piney, Big Tavern,
Little Tavern, Gasconade, Bear Creek, Roubidoux—down
and down into my worn, God-ridden home, the little town
I couldn't wait to leave.

Acknowledgments

I am grateful to the following journals, in which these poems first appeared, sometimes in slightly different versions:

Apalachee Review: "Third Day of the Year"
Caesura: "Rapture"
California Quarterly: "Sunset on the 38 Geary," "Time"
Chattahoochee Review: "Dark, Starry, Sticky Night: Missouri"
The Gettysburg Review: "The Market in Limogne,"
    "One Thousand, Two Thousand," "Ripeness"
KYSO Flash: "Cigarettes," "Dog Days"
Miramar Poetry Journal: "Going Back to Big Spring,"
    "The Journey of the Artist," "RSVP"
Pearl: "Another Thing Done Wrong"
Perfume River: "Street Trees of San Francisco"
Prairie Schooner: "Sunny Morning, February"
The Sun: "Back Home," "Three Weeks After"

"Early Beauty" appeared in the chapbook *Constant Lover* (Protean Press, 2001).

"Environmental Poetry Festival" and "For Nancy" appeared in the chapbook *World Made of Desire* (Protean Press, 2014).

"Why We Sleep" appeared in the chapbook *This Is Mine* (Protean Press, 2004).

"What to Remember" appeared in the anthology *The Other Side of the Postcard* (City Lights Foundation, 2004).

"Wild Poppies" appeared in the anthology *Swallow Dance* (Silver Birch Press, 2014).

"Cigarettes" was reprinted in *KYSO Flash Anthology*, Volume 1 (KYSO Flash, 2014).

"Dark, Starry, Sticky Night: Missouri" was reprinted in *A Dream of Summer* (Beacon Press, 2004).

"For Nancy" was reprinted in *Swallow Dance* (Silver Birch Press, 2014).

"Walking Song" was published (as "Walking Poem") as a *Pocket Poem* for the Second National Poem-in-Your-Pocket Day, 2009.

"Why We Sleep" was printed as a broadside (Protean Press, 2004).

About the Author

Carolyn Miller grew up in the Missouri Ozarks, where she was baptized in the Roubidoux River at the age of eight. Today, she lives in a Romeo and Juliet flat on the Hyde Street cable-car line in San Francisco, where she writes, paints, and works as a freelance writer/editor. Her books of poetry are *After Cocteau* and *Light, Moving*, both from Sixteen Rivers Press, and four limited-edition letterpress chapbooks from Protean Press. Her poems have been featured on *Poetry Daily* and *The Writer's Almanac* and have appeared in *The Gettysburg Review*, *The Southern Review*, *Prairie Schooner*, and *The Georgia Review*, among other journals, as well as in several anthologies, including Garrison Keillor's *Good Poems: American Places*. Her honors include the James Boatwright III Award for Poetry from *Shenandoah* and the Rainmaker Award from *Zone 3*.

CPSIA information can be obtained
at www.ICGtesting.com
Printed in the USA
LVHW052118161118
597207LV00002B/170/P

9 780997 666656